S0-AIM-386

EDGE BOOKS™

Secret America

Secret American Places

From UFO Crash Sites to Government Hideouts

by Nel Yomtov

Consultant:
Jessica Martin, PhD
History Department
University of Colorado, Boulder

Mankato, Minnesota

Edge Books are published by Capstone Press,
151 Good Counsel Drive, P.O. Box 669, Mankato, Minnesota 56002.
www.capstonepress.com

Printed in the United States of America

Books published by Capstone Press are manufactured with paper containing at least 10 percent post-consumer waste.

Library of Congress Cataloging-in-Publication Data

Yomtov, Nelson.

Secret American places: from UFO crash sites to government hideouts / by Nel Yomtov

p. cm. — (Edge books. Secret America)

Includes bibliographical references and index.

Summary: "Describes a variety of secret and mysterious places in the United States" — Provided by publisher.

ISBN 978-1-4296-3359-8 (library binding)

1. United States — History, Local — Juvenile literature. 2. Historic sites — United States — Juvenile literature. 3. Curiosities and wonders — United States — Juvenile literature. 4. Secrecy — United States — Miscellanea — Juvenile literature. I.Title.

E159.Y66 2010

973 — dc22 2009001165

Editorial Credits

Kathryn Clay, editor; Tracy Davies, designer; Eric Gohl, media researcher

Photo Credits

Alamy/Robert Estall Photo Agency, 8, 9; Alamy/Tom Till, 23; AP Images/Charlie Riedel, 12; DVIC/TSGT Cedric H. Rudisill, USAF, 21; Getty Images Inc./James Aylott, 24; Getty Images Inc./National Geographic/Albert Moldvay, 20; Getty Images Inc./Time & Life Pictures/William F. Campbell, 10; Glenn Campbell, 26; iStockphoto/Dave Roboin, cover (middle), 14; Newscom/KRT Photos/Great Lakes Shipwreck Museum via Duluth News Tribune, 17; Photodisc, 18; Photo Researchers, Inc/David Hardy, cover (left), 6; Riverbluff Cave/Matt Forir, 13; Shutterstock/Cobalt Moon Design, (patriotic background design element); Shutterstock/David Majestic, 16; Shutterstock/digitalife, (banners design element); Shutterstock/Janaka, (paper design element); Shutterstock/Jeffrey M. Frank, 22; Shutterstock/photoBeard, 7; Shutterstock/PKruger, (cobbled road design element); Shutterstock/Sergey Kandakov, (black paper design element); Shutterstock/Sibrikov Valery, (old paper design element); Shutterstock/SipaPhoto, cover (right), 4, 27; Shutterstock/velora, (wax seal design element); Wikipedia/X51, 28

The author dedicates this book to Nancy and Jess.

Table of Contents

Uncovering America's Secret Places

Secret places are hidden away in every corner of America. Most people don't even know these strange locations exist. Some of these places are dangerous. Others are downright scary. All of the places have one thing in common. Each is filled with great mystery.

Were alien bodies really recovered from a UFO crash in Roswell, New Mexico? Does the U.S. government have an underground hiding place it goes to during emergencies? What secrets lay hidden in the curious burial mounds of the Midwest?

Prepare yourself for plenty of thrills and surprises. Our journey into secret America begins now.

1

A UFO Crash Site?

Many people are convinced a UFO landed in a field near Roswell, New Mexico, in 1947.

No one doubts that something crashed in Roswell, New Mexico, on July 7, 1947. But people disagree on what actually crashed. Some believe it was an alien spacecraft. They say alien bodies were found at the site.

Army officials first said the object was a flying disk. Later they said it was only a weather balloon. Not everyone was convinced, but interest in the crash soon faded.

About 30 years later, Army Major Jesse Marcel said he handled wreckage from the UFO crash in Roswell. He also said the government was hiding the truth. But he had no real proof.

In the 1990s, U.S. government officials said the weather balloon was specially made to find enemy bombs. They said the bodies recovered were just test dummies. But plenty of people still aren't sure. Tourists visit Roswell each year to investigate the crash site for themselves.

Edge Fact:
Some people claim that studies of alien wreckage led to the invention of lasers.

autopsy — an examination performed after someone dies to find the cause of death

Alien Autopsy

In 1995, Ray Santilli claimed he had a film of an alien **autopsy**. He said the alien body came from Roswell. Millions of people viewed the film and believed it was proof that aliens exist. Santilli later admitted that the film was a re-creation. He said the original had been damaged.

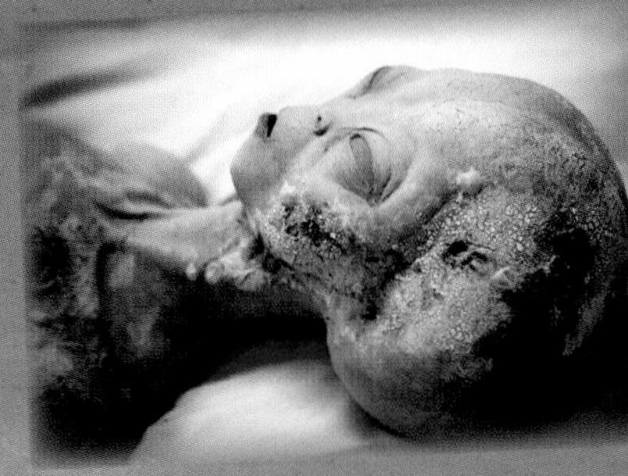

2

America's Stonehenge

A narrow entrance leads to an underground room called the Watch House.

Edge Fact:

Jonathan Pattee discovered Mystery Hill in the 1820s. According to rumor, Pattee hid illegal liquor in the stone chambers.

The Sacrificial Stone

The Sacrificial Stone is a large, flat rock at Mystery Hill. The rock has a deep groove in it. Many people believe victims were sacrificed here during religious ceremonies. The groove would have allowed the victims' blood to run off.

When it comes to Mystery Hill, researchers agree that it is truly an incredible mystery. Located near North Salem, New Hampshire, Mystery Hill is made up of stone walls, chambers, and secret underground passages. Nearby stones are covered with strange carvings.

There are many theories about Mystery Hill. One idea is that Irish monks landed there in 900. They may have built Mystery Hill as a church. Other people compare the rock formations to those built by ancient people at Stonehenge, England. Like Stonehenge, the rocks at Mystery Hill can track movements of the sun and moon.

It's possible the caves at Mystery Hill were also used as stops on the Underground Railroad. Scientists found chains that may have been left by runaway slaves.

3

Mount Weather

Tall fences and armed guards protect Mount Weather.

On September 11, 2001, terrorists flew planes into the World Trade Center and the Pentagon. Moments later, U.S. government officials were in planes too. They were going to Mount Weather, the federal government's secret hiding place.

Mount Weather is an underground base located about 48 miles (77 kilometers) from Washington, D.C., near Berryville, Virginia. It was first used in the 1890s as a place to observe the weather. Weather balloons and kites were launched from the mountain peaks. Millions of dollars were spent during the 1950s to turn the area into a secret **bunker.** Today Mount Weather has offices, sidewalks, a cafeteria, and a hospital. Everything is underground.

Few people know what goes on at Mount Weather. Even top government officials are not allowed to know. Maybe military information is stored there. War preparation may be carried out there. Mount Weather might even hold private information on U.S. citizens.

Security around Mount Weather increased after the September 11, 2001, attacks. Anyone driving too slowly near the site may be pulled over and questioned.

bunker — an underground shelter

Edge Fact:

The door to Mount Weather's underground site is 5 feet (1.5 meters) thick. It weighs more than 30 tons (27 metric tons).

Unwanted Attention

In 1974, an airplane crashed near Mount Weather. The crash created unwanted attention for the underground facility. Reporters began asking questions, but the government revealed few details.

4

A Cave of Clues

Scientists study the large rock formations found in Riverbluff Cave.

Edge Fact:

Cave researchers found a 630,000-year-old mammoth bone inside Riverbluff Cave. It is one of the oldest fossils ever found in North America.

Imagine accidentally uncovering one of America's most important **geological** finds! A group of construction workers in Missouri did just that in 2001. They discovered Riverbluff Cave while blowing up rock for a new road.

According to researchers, the cave is at least 1 million years old. No living creature had been in this hidden cave for at least 55,000 years.

Riverbluff Cave is a gold mine for researchers. They have found tracks made by peccaries, a type of Ice Age pig. Claw prints made by a giant bear were found 14 feet (4 meters) off the ground. That's twice as high as any modern bear can reach!

Riverbluff Cave reveals clues about life on earth thousands of years ago. As work continues at the cave, we can only imagine the incredible discoveries still to come.

geological — relating to the study of Earth's rock and soil

Dung Discovery

Animal dung has been found inside Riverbluff Cave. Preserved dung is very rare. Researchers use the dung to find out what kinds of foods prehistoric animals ate.

5

Mount Shasta

Northern California's Mount Shasta rises to 14,000 feet (4,270 meters).

Could this mountain be a landing site for UFOs? Did ancient people live here after their continent sank? These ideas may sound silly. But they are just some of the things people believe about the mysterious Mount Shasta.

One legend suggests that Mount Shasta is full of tunnels used to hide UFOs. Nearby residents have also reported seeing strange lights shining from the mountain. A hiker claimed to see a fighter jet fly into the mountain. He said the mountain opened up like a door, and the plane flew inside.

The most famous legend claims Mount Shasta is home to the people of Lemuria. In 1905, Frederick Spencer Oliver wrote a book about the Lemurians. He said these strange people traveled to Mount Shasta after their continent sank.

After Oliver's book was published, some people claimed to see Lemurians on Mount Shasta. But most people think these stories are untrue.

Edge Fact:
Some people claim to have seen Bigfoot on Mount Shasta.

dormant — not active

Ready to Erupt

Mount Shasta is a stratovolcano. It has a tall cone made of hardened lava and volcanic ash. This **dormant** volcano will likely erupt in the future. Unfortunately, no one knows when that will be. It last erupted 200 years ago.

6

The Great Lakes Triangle

More than 100 lighthouses guide the way for ships traveling in the Great Lakes.

Most people know about the Bermuda Triangle in the Atlantic Ocean. But there's a place where even more strange disappearances occur. It's called the Great Lakes Triangle.

The Great Lakes are Lake Erie, Lake Huron, Lake Michigan, Lake Ontario, and Lake Superior. They border the United States and Canada.

A Mysterious Wreck

In November 1975, the freighter *Edmund Fitzgerald* was sailing on Lake Superior. The *Anderson* traveled 10 miles (16 kilometers) behind it. The crew was tracking the *Fitzgerald* on radar.

Heavy snowfall and large waves made travel difficult for both ships. Suddenly the *Fitzgerald* disappeared from radar. The wreck was located, but no survivors were found. Some people blame the weather for the disappearance. Others think faulty equipment might be to blame. No theories have been proven.

Hundreds of ships have sunk in these waters. Many airplanes have also crashed into the lakes. But no one knows what caused the wrecks.

Ship crews have reported memory loss. Planes flying over the Great Lakes have lost power with no explanation.

Some people think there is a magnetic field over the lakes. A strong magnetic force might interrupt electrical equipment. Others say aliens kidnap the ships and planes. UFO sightings have been reported in the area. Scientists are still looking for an answer to the mystery.

7 The Pentagon

The Pentagon building in Arlington, Virginia, holds all of the U.S. Department of Defense offices.

In 1941, World War II (1939–1945) was raging in Europe. At the time, workers for the U.S. War Department were spread out in 17 buildings. A new building was needed to bring everyone together. The solution was to build the Pentagon.

Officials said the building would cost $35 million. But the final cost was about $83 million. That's because the original plans only called for three floors. The building plans changed when Pearl Harbor was attacked on December 7, 1941. The war department then needed even more room to plan war operations. A fourth and fifth level were added to the plans. Two more levels were hidden underground.

Edge Fact:

The Pentagon's five-sided shape was the result of space limitations. A military training field, roads, and a railway surround the building.

Today more than 23,000 people work at the Pentagon. This includes both military and **civilian** workers. Many of the workers are accountants, secretaries, and maintenance crews. But some people at the Pentagon spend their days planning secret military operations. These members of the Department of Defense decide how to defend the United States against enemy attacks.

civilian — a person who is not in the military

The Pentagon offers group tours for people wanting to check out this amazing place. Visitors can see memorials and war displays throughout the building. But don't expect to see any top secret military operations being planned. Strictly off-limits is the National Military Command Center, which keeps a constant watch on the world. Workers there receive reports from everywhere on earth.

The Pentagon is one of the most protected places in America, and visitors are closely watched. A police force called the Pentagon Force Protection Agency (PFPA) is in charge of security. There's also an emergency SWAT team. Some people say that the Pentagon has a missile system to shoot down attacking planes. But there is no proof the system exists.

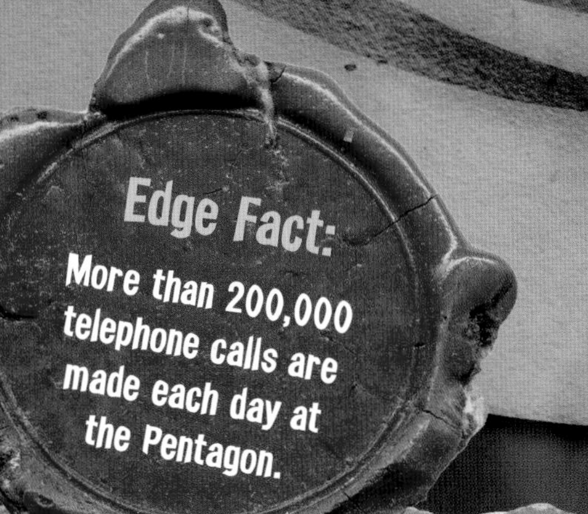

The Pentagon under Attack

The Pentagon is a symbol of national defense. For this reason, it has been a target for terrorists. In its lifetime, the Pentagon has been violently attacked twice.

In 1972, a group called the Weather Underground planted a bomb in a bathroom. The explosion blew out part of a wall, but no one was injured.

On September 11, 2001, terrorists flew a plane into the Pentagon. More than 180 people were killed. The Pentagon was badly damaged, but repairs began immediately. Repair costs were more than $500 million.

Indian Burial Mounds

Mound B is an Etowah Indian burial mound built in Georgia between 1000 and 1500.

When settlers arrived in America, they found huge mounds of earth. Most of the mounds were in the Ohio and Mississippi River Valleys. The mounds were shaped like pyramids, snakes, eagles, and humans. Researchers found tobacco pipes, copper, and skeletons in the mounds.

People began to wonder what the mounds were. Some said the mounds were the remains of the mythical city of Atlantis. Today we know the structures are burial mounds built by American Indians.

In Cahokia, Illinois, there are about 100 mounds, including the largest mound in North America. Monk's Mound is 100 feet (30 meters) tall and 700 feet (213 meters) wide. Researchers believe the home of a tribal leader once stood on the mound. Another burial mound in Cahokia had about 300 bodies in it, including one of a male ruler. Some researchers think the other bodies were sacrificed to serve the ruler in the afterlife.

Edge Fact:
Monk's Mound has a larger base than the Egyptian pyramids.

One Big Snake

The most famous Indian burial mound is the Great Serpent Mound in southern Ohio. The mound is about 3 feet (.9 meter) high and 1,300 feet (396 meters) long. The serpent's mouth is open, and it looks like it's swallowing an egg-shaped object. The Adena tribe made the mound about 2,000 years ago.

9

Area 51

Few people have seen what goes on inside the secret buildings at Area 51.

For being a secret place, Area 51 is very famous. Some people believe the government keeps UFOs and alien bodies at this Nevada Air Force base. Whether that's true or not, one thing is certain. There's something very mysterious going on there.

Edge Fact:
Area 51 does not appear on public maps. The official government map of the area only shows a mine that was abandoned years ago.

In the 1950s, Area 51 was set up as a secret test site for military spy planes. Soon neighbors saw low-flying objects and bright lights. That's when the UFO rumors started. Even today, some people are convinced that U.S. government workers brought alien wreckage from Roswell, New Mexico, to Area 51.

Faking It

In 1989, Bob Lazar claimed he was a scientist who had studied UFOs near Area 51. He said he had read alien autopsy reports. Researchers quickly discovered that Lazar never worked near Area 51. He also wasn't a scientist. But it was too late. Many people already believed him. Soon thousands of people began traveling to Area 51 to get a closer look.

The government works hard to keep Area 51 a secret. Signs warn visitors to stay away. Photography is not allowed. Security cameras and motion detectors keep track of people driving nearby. Private security guards nicknamed Cammo Dudes patrol the area in white vehicles. The guards are armed with powerful weapons.

Cammo Dudes guard the area around Area 51 to keep out unwanted visitors.

Edge Fact:
Some people think experiments in weather control and time travel are conducted at Area 51.

UFO Capital of the World

The closest town to Area 51 is Rachel, Nevada. The town is 25 miles (40 kilometers) from the base and has a population of fewer than 100 people. Because the town is so close to Area 51, Rachel is nicknamed the UFO capital of the world.

NELLIS BOMBING AND GUNNERY RANGE
RESTRICTED AREA
NO TRESPASSING
BEYOND THIS
POINT
PHOTOGRAPHY IS
PROHIBITED
WARNING
Restricted Area

Discovering New Secrets

It's fun to think about the hidden secrets of the world. Throughout America, you'll find thousands of places that hold strange and puzzling secrets. Some of those secrets are true, and others are just legends. The fun is trying to figure out what's fact and what's fiction.

If you want to check out other hidden places in America, start in your own neighborhood. Your trip can begin at your local library. Or you can search the Internet. You'll be amazed at some of the secrets you'll uncover about places near your home. Good luck hunting!

Glossary

autopsy (AW-top-see) — an examination performed on a dead body to find the cause of death

bunker (BUHNG-kuhr) — an underground shelter that protects people from bomb attacks and gunfire

civilian (si-VIL-yuhn) — a person who is not in the military

dormant (DOR-muhnt) — not active; dormant volcanoes have not erupted for many years.

dung (DUHNG) — solid waste from animals

fossil (FAH-suhl) — the remains or traces of an animal or plant from millions of years ago preserved as rock

geological (jee-oh-LAH-ji-kuhl) — relating to the study of Earth's rock and soil

monk (MUHNGK) — a man who lives in a religious community and promises to devote his life to his religion

prehistoric (pree-hi-STOR-ik) — belonging to a time before history was recorded in written form

sacrifice (SAK-ruh-fice) — to kill an animal or person in order to honor a god

Read More

DeMolay, Jack. *UFOs: The Roswell Incident.* Jr. Graphic Mysteries. New York: PowerKids Press, 2007.

Harrison, David L. *Cave Detectives: Unraveling the Mystery of an Ice Age Cave.* San Francisco: Chronicle Books, 2007.

Sievert, Terri. *UFOs.* The Unexplained. Mankato, Minn.: Capstone Press, 2005.

Internet Sites

FactHound offers a safe, fun way to find Internet sites related to this book. All of the sites on FactHound have been researched by our staff.

Here's all you do:

Visit *www.facthound.com*

WWW.FACTHOUND.COM®

FactHound will fetch the best sites for you!

Index